Self Love

A 28 Day Guided Journal

Claudia Roth

ISBN 978-1-9163507-0-0

Image Credits: Cover image Shutterstock; inside pages Shutterstock and Hello Lovely design.

Content development and editor: Petra Mo

Proofreaders: Tim Wrey and Chelsey Baker

Book design and layout by Berenice Smith, Hello Lovely Design

Printed by Ingram Spark

Visit www.soul-luxury.com for more details.

For information about bulk purchases, please contact hello@soul-luxury.com

Disclaimer

This journal is meant to offer encouragement and exploration and does not replace any need for professional therapy. The author/publisher assumes no liability for any negative consequences that any person might experience as a result of using this journal, although that's unlikely. Please seek help if you feel you cannot handle things on your own and/or have continual and lasting negative thoughts.

Welcome

This Self Love Journal
belongs to:

....

Your task is not to seek for love, but merely to seek and find all the barriers within yourself that you have built against it.

Rumi

About this Journal and How to Use it

The Concept and Objective

Journaling is an excellent tool for processing life experiences. It can help us feel less stressed and anxious and to value life more.

This 4-week journal is what is normally referred to as a guided journal. It is structured to guide you, through self-reflection, towards getting to know who you truly are which is - in essence - love.

An invitation to go beyond the material, it offers to take you on a journey from your ego, from self-criticism and feeling of unworthiness to peace and deep joy.

If you are reading these lines you have most likely been on an inner quest for some time, and are now feeling called to deepen your understanding about who you are.

Self Love is a state of being that allows you to connect with life in its fullest sense, and to see that you are life, rather than life being something that is happening to you.

The moment we feel truly worthy of ourselves we can love others too, for whom they are, rather than whom we want them to be. This, in turn, can heal our relationship with others.

Claudia Roth

There is no template, you are the template. Dive in and enjoy the unearthing of you

Trust that you have been guided to hold this journal in your hands, and know that you are invited to move from self to a more intuitive higher self in contact with your soul.

The sacred ritual of daily self-reflection can help lift veils of conditioning and peel away illusory self images. Beneath these veils is Self, which contains everything.

Seeing through the false image of self as limited to a separate body-mind structure is powerful.

Life is a gift, an opportunity for our soul to experience unity as Self, in full awareness.

How to Use this Journal

1 Start with reading this introduction and letting it sink in. Take as much time as you need and then set the date for your Day 1.

2 Each day has a spread with one reflection followed by an assignment. It's best to read the reflection in the morning, and to complete the assignment at the same time or to return to it later in the day. There are two exceptions to this format (Day 19 and 24), which is made clear on those days.

3 Each new 7-day cycle starts with a slightly longer introductory text. Make sure that on those days you have time to read it before moving on to the reflection of the day.

Some Additional Pointers

- Honour yourself and your life enough to commit to the 28 days; it's best not to stop the flow.
- It is very normal, when looking deep within, to feel resistance and to procrastinate. It can be seen as a way to 'protect yourself', to want to abandon the process, but try to stick with it!
- If unable to follow through, do not despair. Put the journal aside and return to it when you feel called to do so. There is no failure, only growth and progress.
- If you don't have an answer to a question, acknowledge that this is OK. You may want to revisit it the next day.
- There is no right or wrong answer. This is your personal journey.
- Stay open to whatever emerges naturally.
- Aim to keep the mind quiet and to allow for free flow writing. This will clear space for your heart, or 'inner voice', to come through uncensored.
- Listening to this inner voice can help you understand what your life experiences are trying to tell you.

This journaling journey has the potential to de-clutter your life of self-images and outdated beliefs that no longer serve you and to awaken you to the potential of connecting to a more expansive sense of self, and Self Love. Your future self will thank you for this journey.

To wake up from this dream is to remember who you truly are; which is nothing but love. Know that *forgiveness* is a key that can open you up to this truth.

Lazo Freeman

Week 1
Ordinary Life - Extraordinary Life

It all starts with observing one's self, which sounds strange, doesn't it?

Because, how can something observe itself?

Ordinary Life - Extraordinary Life

Most likely at some point in the future, your future self will look back at who you are today. Will that future self thank or curse your 'present (today) self' for something that you did in this moment?

This question helps us understand the power of the present moment, in which seeds are being planted. Intention is crucial and today is a perfect day to take a first step, to accept that we don't know where the journey will lead to, and to know that change is the only constant.

The world as we know it today will not be the world of the future, and neither will your future self be the same as your current self.

Accepting change instead of resisting it, and trusting that your challenges are only testing your ability to flow with the change, will help. Radically speaking, this means to surrender to all the apparent paradoxes in life. As you do so, the centre within you may invite you to dissolve into it.

This is where true peace is found, even in the midst of worldly chaos and crisis. And to rest here is the deepest spiritual skill. It is the way of the heart, and the way out of suffering.

Developing the skill to rest in the centre within, also in the midst of chaos, is something that your future self will definitely thank your current self for.

Beneath the zigzagging of life there is an ever-present stillness. This is the pot of gold at the heart of your being.

Can you access it and allow it to guide you?

Day 1: Life is a Maze What is Life?

It might seem, at times, that life is nothing but a constant jumping between 'amazing' and 'a mess', a life of opposites.

There is another way of looking at it - as a maze. Life, in a way, is the chain of choices that we make. Each turn we take matters and the destination will reflect the sum of all the moves of our delicate dance.

Mostly, we have to accept that the outcome of any one decision is an unknown, and that we can either play it safe or take risks. When we play it safe, we tend to look at life as linear. Rationalising our decisions, we allow our minds to stay in charge of our destiny.

Accept the Unknown

Right now, what is the choice that you want to make but are afraid to make?

> *Sometimes, we need to take risks in order to discover the pot of gold at the heart of our being, the ever-present stillness that we truly are.*
> *– Claudia Roth*

What excuses are you making? Excuses are OK, and it might just be that you need more time, yet bringing awareness to it all has the potential to help you understand what is holding you back from following your heart. What are you afraid of? Is there a pattern in your life regarding these fears?

List any recurring fears, behaviours or patterns that keep cropping up.

You are invited to make notes.

Day 2: Silencing the Inner Critic

Inner progress is often categorised by subtle shifts in awareness and 'Aha!' moments. For those of us who are wired to wanting to make progress, such moments help us along.

Sometimes much time passes without a single such moment. Our inner critic might complain and tell us that we are at a standstill. This will only make us feel impatient and frustrated and serves no purpose.

It's worth remembering that on a very subtle level our conditioned mind may not yet be sensitive enough to sense that progress is happening. We have curated and reinforced our personality over decades. Mistaking it for who we are, we hang onto it for dear life. And as we start to grow out of old habit-patterns, the ego tends to fight back even more intensely. Then we need to be especially patient with ourselves.

It's all too easy to be self critical. Instead, take some time to find your inner Cheerleader – you might be surprised! – Claudia Roth

Acknowledge Your Regrets and Progress

Take a deep breath and look back at your life. Acknowledge your progress as well as regrets and perceived mistakes, knowing that these, too, have helped you progress.

Are you the same as you were 5 years ago? 10 years ago? 20 years ago? What do you see has changed? And what has stayed the same about you?

Allowing whatever wants to come to mind, make notes here.

Day 3: The Opinions of Others

Generally we give too much power not only to our inner critic but also to the opinions of others. We are constantly asking ourselves, “what will she or he think if I do this or that?” This has consequences.

When we are too obsessed with what others think of us, reacting takes constant time and energy, so much so that we are not able to hear our own inner voice.

The moment we free ourselves from outside voices we create inner space to hear our soul’s desire.

In the language of the soul there is no comparison and no judgment. There is only love, joy and freedom.

There is nobody better at being you than YOU. – Claudia Roth

Reclaim Your Life

Ask yourself:

Whose opinions are stopping me from confidently walking my own unique life-maze path?

How can I distinguish between good and bad advice?

How can I listen less to others and more to myself?

You are invited to write down your thoughts.

Day 4: No Pain, No Gain?

There is a lot of talk about staying positive. However staying positive for the sake of staying positive hinders true progress. To progress in this lifetime we need to look beneath the surface, beyond our self-images. We need to embrace our shadow side, which might be painful. Then it's worthwhile remembering that pain has the potential to transform into compassion, Self Love and Light.

We tend to not question our life's path as long as all is 'going well' according to our mind's plan. Yet in an unexpected situation we feel overwhelmed by emotions. Feeling overwhelmed, we easily get lost in the drama, a seeming wilderness of thoughts and emotions. We feel overwhelmed by emotions of fear, grief or anxiety.

No pressure, no diamonds. No pressure, no pearl.

No pain, no gain. No cocoon, no beautiful butterfly.

It's in the uncertain and dark and unclear and broken times that we learn who we really are and what we are capable of. – Kemmy Nola

Connect to Your Inner Guide

Take a deep breath and recall a time when you distracted yourself by allowing your fears and self-pity to find expression and let them out in some way.

At that time of distraction or repression of feelings, was there perhaps something that you wanted to keep hidden from yourself and/or others? If so, is it possible to pinpoint what it was exactly?

Try to remember if there was also an inner voice of compassion speaking to you at the time. What was it trying to tell you?

You are invited to make notes.

When you resist and actively try to escape hardship, you risk missing a turning towards Self Love. – Claudia Roth

Day 5: Vulnerability is Strength

We are all steeped in patterns. Some of them we are not even aware of, and they might be running our lives.

Some patterns we are very aware of, but they seem impossible to break. Then, if we look deep within ourselves we might understand that it is because we don't want to. We like what we have shaped ourselves to become.

> *The wound is the place where the Light enters you. – Rumi*

Having invested so much time and effort, we don't want to see it all wasted. And yet, suddenly we are called to let go.

We may find ourselves up against something that we just can't accept. It could be something that we label as a weakness.

Weakness often boils down to our mind interpreting a feeling of ourselves as being inferior to somebody else.

We spend a considerable amount of energy on hiding our perceived weaknesses from others; energy that is wasted.

Accept Your 'Weaknesses'

Name your weaknesses. Feel into them, acknowledging any pain or shame they bring to the surface. Done with an open and sincere heart, this may relieve you of their burden.

What situations or people make you feel most vulnerable? Write down your feelings.

Day 6: Breaking Down the Illusion

Our default mode is often to do what is expected of us. If we live like this, without questioning if it's in line with what we truly want, our feeling happy and fulfilled is likely an illusion. Why? We may think that we are happy when we are meeting others' expectations or making them happy, but is this true happiness?

In the early years of life, most of us have no concept of having a real choice when it comes to how we live our lives. Also later in life, many of us live as if on autopilot.

> Numb the dark and you numb the light. – Brené Brown

Then, at some point, often triggered by difficulties and questioning, we may wake up and realise that we do have a say. That's when we start to take ownership of our life, beyond ego and conditioning and dare to be different. And that's when we see clearly, that by being vulnerable, not outwardly 'perfect' or 'strong' we can open up to self-discovery.

Question Your Tradition

You probably started out navigating through life by following the dictates of your upbringing and your environment.

Take a deep breath and consider your life now. Are you adhering to the rules of the past or are you following your happiness?

You are invited to make some truly honest notes here.

You are here on earth to experience the blissful state that is your birthright. – Claudia Roth

Day 7: Four Profound Questions

To truly accept any situation, no matter how difficult, is a skill that for most people takes practice.

For each individual, getting there will be a different process.

Looking back on our lives, we may conclude that we have 'done wrong' yet to see that there truly is no 'wrong' is a priceless gift.

> *Life is only a reflection of what we allow ourselves to see. – Trudy Symeonakis Vesotsky*

Understanding that we do our best in each moment, we can forgive ourselves if needed. The invitation to self-discovery can come in the shape of a major life event or a subtle knowing.

If accepted, it can help us drop emotional burdens and deceptive self images.

Ask Yourself – In Acceptance

Does my life have a purpose?

What is the highest I am capable of?

How can I contribute to making the world a better place?

Where and what is my path in all this?

You are invited to write your contemplations. Answer these 4 questions:

1 Does my life have a purpose?

2 What is the highest I am capable of?

3 How can I contribute to making the world a better place?

4 Where and what is my path in all this?

Our deepest fear is not that we are inadequate. Our deepest fear is that we are powerful beyond measure. – Marianne Williamson

Not one thing in the universe has a single inherent meaning. The meaning of a thing is in the mind of the perceiver and not in the object of *perception.*

Mooji

Week 2
The 'Who Am I?' Question

Until we seriously consider the question 'Who Am I?' we stay on the surface. This question can take us to a direct knowing, if we manage to rid ourselves of preconceived ideas.

The 'Who Am I?' Question

The evolution of consciousness can be said to move along four inter-connected, fluid and overlapping lines that can also be described as states of being, starting with the unconscious self:

1 Unconscious self: This links to our body's automatic functioning, such as breathing or a wound healing. It can also be said to signify the state of being before we form an idea of ourselves as being separate. As children, up to a point, we are not aware of being separate, and this state can also be referred to as 'our inner child'. Unconscious self also signifies the depth that our mind may not be aware of or want to accept, and we do need to evolve to become conscious.

2 Conditioned self: Seeing ourselves as separate individuals we enter into duality and suffering. We falsely believe that "we are what we think and do and feel" and that we (conditioned self) are "in control". Focus is on fulfilling desires and wants, especially in the material realm, but conditioned self is limited.

3 Higher self: When ingrained beliefs, patterns and behaviours i.e. conditioned self, is seen through and asked to move to the backseat, the bigger picture is revealed, as is the possibility of infinite creativity limited only by our imagination. The higher self is the part of you that knows, sees, and is directly

The moon is a reminder that no matter
what phase I am in I'm still whole.

TheMindsJournal.com

connected to soul, our eternal essence that has to some extent designed the experiences of this lifetime.

4 Oneness/Truth (a.k.a. All That Is, The Unified Field, Pure Consciousness): Here, there is only the "now" and incomparable endless bliss, peace and unconditional love. Consciously one with all of creation, one is in a state of being beyond mind, intellect and ego. It can't be described, only known, but we all glimpse it when something "takes our breath away" or "time stood still" - we are not separate from the experience.

While we evolve from the lower realm to the upper realm, we vacillate in our progress based on our conditioning, beliefs and desires, and also based on 'something else', an inexplicable force. The integration of perception and embracing of parallel realities must become our daily exercise, as it is by simultaneously holding multiple viewpoints and multiple perspectives that we begin to encompass the truth of our world.

The thought 'Who am I?' will destroy all other thoughts, and like the stick used for stirring the funeral pyre, it will itself be burnt up in the end. Then, there will be Self-realization. When other thoughts arise, one should not pursue them but should diligently enquire:

'To whom do they occur?'

It does not matter how many thoughts arise. As each thought arises one should enquire with alertness, 'To whom has this thought arisen?' The answer that would emerge would be 'to me'. Thereupon if one enquires 'Who am I?' the mind will go back to its source, and the thought that arose will subside.

Ramana Maharshi

Day 8: Troubles, Tantrums...

The word joy doesn't imply that everything is easy. As we tap into the deep peace that is always there, beneath any troubles or tantrums of the ego demanding that life should be a certain way, we become one with the kind of joy that doesn't depend on any outer events.

> *To be a star, you must shine your own light, follow your path, and don't worry about the darkness, for that is when the stars shine brightest.* – Ralph Waldo Emerson

Connected to my soul, I live out the experience of the Truth of 'Who I am', which is peace, joy and love beyond my physical body, my thoughts and my emotions.

In this space I am liberated to undo whatever falsehood my conditioned beliefs have imprinted on me.

This allows space for a version of 'I' that is able to live without anxiety in this seemingly chaotic world.

...and Transformations

Remember a time in your life when you faced some hardship. How big does it seem to you now, compared to when you were in the midst of it happening? What would it have taken for you to keep calm in the midst of that storm?

You are invited to make some notes here.

You don't need to sit in a cave to live a life in alignment with the Truth. Truth is here, in modern life too.

Being in the flow of change and transformation, life becomes joy. – Claudia Roth

Day 9: Expecting Nothing

Being alone and immersed in one's own presence is a powerful experience that has nothing to do with loneliness. Rather, in this state one is in a better space to meet life's challenges more wisely.

> *We have to develop spiritual stamina so when a problem occurs we don't react out of emotion but out of wisdom. – Unknown*

Someone said that every person we meet is either a lesson or a blessing, but what if the biggest lessons are our biggest blessings? This might sound crazy, and yet, what if it's true?

'Whenever you expect anything from others, appreciation or anything else, you are not being independent, and this is bound to bring you down. You must say, "I don't expect anything from others, whatever I need to do, I will keep on doing it." *Sri Sri Ravi Shankar*

Spend Three Minutes in Awe

Give yourself the gift of spending three minutes of your life turning your attention to the miracles around you, contemplating everything you see.

This exercise is inspired by Wayne Dyer

Write down for what you are grateful.

Spending three minutes every day to appreciate, in gratitude, all that surrounds you will help you focus your life in awe. – Claudia Roth

Day 10: A New World is Born

We are still at the relative beginning of a time of evolutionary change. In only a few years time, likely nothing will be the same as it is now. We are seeing a rapid rise in Artificial Intelligence. It is likely to hugely impact our society, and is developing so quickly that it gives an idea of the enormity of the shift that we are in.

Some see a transition from traditional industries to an economy based on values that honour spiritual and ecological well-being, with old structures and hierarchies falling by the wayside.

Others see only that the globe is in crisis, with no positive outcome in sight, and need only turn to the traditional news outlets to confirm this impression.

> No man ever steps in the same river twice, for it's not the same river and he's not the same man.
> – Heraclitus

Allow Yourself to be Reborn

Sit quietly, undisturbed, and listen within.

How do you feel about the world right now?

Are you a current affairs junkie expecting the worst, or do you trust in the universe? If it is the former, would it be possible to engineer a u-turn, if only to feel better?

What would you like to change?

Write down what comes to mind.

The future is unknown; acknowledging that we are right in the middle of a major evolutionary upgrade can help us accept the current challenges. – Claudia Roth

Day 11: Inner World, True Self

We all strive for happiness. Most of us find it to be elusive - here one moment, gone the next. It's only by seeing that happiness can't be found outside of ourselves - not in status, financial success, likes or shares on social media, not even in relationships - that something can shift.

Abandoning the pursuit of the outer and surrendering to the peace and unconditional love that rest in our hearts, we can still live an ordinary (or extraordinary!) modern and busy life. Even more can be achieved staying connected, as we don't lose ourselves in the wilderness of thoughts, beliefs and emotions that are due to striving.

> *Harmony is dependent upon a recognition of difference and a willingness to hold one's own truth intact in its presence.*
> – Oneness through Rasha

Inner and Outer – One

To experiment with opening up to guidance and seeing that the inner is connected to the outer, try this: consider the books next to your bed or in your bookshelf. If there is one with a spiritual angle, great, yet any will do, even a crime thriller. Open the book to the page which you feel 'randomly' drawn to. What is written on the page? Is it telling you anything? What?

How does it relate to your life or inner world now?

The idea of this exercise is to check the hypothesis that there are no coincidences in life and that guidance and help are always at hand if we keep an alert and open mind.

You are invited to make some notes here.

Day 12: Expectations are Limiting

Often, we let the expectations of others lead us towards behaviour that doesn't serve us.

Also our own expectations can be limiting. If that is the case, it might help to remember that to be in flow with life does not mean that only what we want to happen does, it means to accept whatever happens.

When you are in service to yourself and are committed to personally evolving and changing, you uplift everyone around you. That is service. Service is not going out and martyring yourself and saying, 'I'm going to save you.' Service is doing the work yourself and living in such a way that everyone you touch is affected by your journey. – Healing Energy Tool

Plunge Into the Unknown

Read aloud to yourself:

I plunge into the unknown. I free myself of knowing, with the understanding that trust is my friend and guide, and that Love is who I am. In trust and surrender I plunge into the freedom of the unknown.

Expecting nothing but what life is serving up for me, moment by moment, I flow with life. – Claudia Roth

How does it feel? Does it feel scary or joyful, or maybe both?

Describe your emotions:

As long as you cling to the idea of the way 'life is supposed to be', your life circumstances will continue to reflect a perspective that sees itself as the effect of circumstances beyond your control. – The Wisdom of Oneness through Rasha

Day 13: That is not You

Looking into the mirror, what do we see?

The wall, the mirror, the image, the reflection, the eyes, the gaze... is that me? Who or what am I?

Am I my name, my upbringing, or my profession?

Can I be said to be an unchanging entity moving through life?

Can my life be said to be an entity, a thing?

Or is it the steady or unsteady flow of what is perceived by my mind?

Am I the perceiver?

Each moment is all that is; no before and no after.

You are Life

Take a meditative walk. Be the witness. Stop and take in the scene, become one with it. Become one with life.

What does it mean for you, to be one with life?

> Nothing that you experience is caused by anything outside of you. You experience only the effects of your own choice. – Shanti Christo Foundation

If you feel resistance or even anger at this question, what might this resistance be telling you?

Write down your reflections.

Day 14: Beyond Intellect

The sages say: 'You are not your body or your thoughts, nor your emotions.'

But then, what are we?

Our true potential lies beyond the intellect.

Naturally our intellect can't grasp this.

Limited by our beliefs and conditioning, most of us remain attached to the dramas of our lives.

As long as experiences are perceived as being positive or negative, making us crave or feel aversion, we remain the prisoners of our illusion of separation.

Like this, we are out of tune with reality as it is.

What is It?

Watch out for intellect, because it knows so much it knows nothing and leaves you hanging upside down, mouthing knowledge as your heart falls out of your mouth. – Anne Sexton

Sit in a quiet spot without any disturbance. Contemplate deeply on the questions:

'Who, or what, is aware that I am thinking?'

'What 'hears' my thoughts?'

If it is 'me' hearing 'my' thoughts and being shocked by my thoughts, there is an issue, right?

Maybe my true seat is as that which hears?

Make some notes here, if you feel able to do so (or simply contemplate what your awareness wants to tell you).

Interlude: My Soul has a Hat

by Mario de Andrade

I counted my years

and realized that I have

less time to live by,

than I have lived so far.

I feel like a child who won a pack of candies: at first he ate them with pleasure

but when he realized that there was little left, he began to taste them intensely.

I have no time for endless meetings

where the statutes, rules, procedures and internal regulations are discussed,

knowing that nothing will be done.

I no longer have the patience

to stand absurd people who,

despite their chronological age,

have not grown up.

My time is too short:

I want the essence;

my spirit is in a hurry.

I do not have much candy

in the package anymore.

I want to live next to humans,

very realistic people who know

how to laugh at their mistakes,

who are not inflated by their own triumphs

and who take responsibility for their actions.

In this way, human dignity is defended

and we live in truth and honesty.

It is the essentials that make life useful.

I want to surround myself with people

who know how to touch the hearts of those whom hard strokes of life

have learned to grow with sweet touches of the soul.

Yes, I'm in a hurry.

I'm in a hurry to live with the intensity that only maturity can give.

I do not intend to waste any of the remaining desserts.

I am sure they will be exquisite,

much more than those eaten so far.

My goal is to reach the end satisfied

and at peace with my loved ones and my conscience.

We have two lives

and the second begins when you realize
you only have one.

I AM the divine design... here on this planet, with a purpose to love humanity. I love the way my path is defined and I adore the way my soul is designed...

I accept myself and the resources around as the way it is, for this is where I need to start with a vision to reach a point destined for me.

Thank you God for what I AM

Nimisha Rattan

Week 3
Becoming the Witness of Your Life

As one says it is 'my life', who does it belong to? Can I observe it rather than be carried along by its currents?

Becoming the Witness of Your Life

Imagine yourself to be a little behind or above things, looking at them taking place however not doing anything yourself.

To be the witness, or observer, means to be someone who looks on and does not act.

When the mind is very quiet you can withdraw a little in this way from circumstances and look at things as though a spectator, not participating in the action.

This gives you a great detachment, quietude and a very precise sense of the value of things, because it cuts the attachment to action.

When you know how to do this yourself, when you can withdraw and watch yourself acting, you have the potential to learn many things about yourself.

When you are all mixed up and take part in the action, you do not observe yourself acting; you don't know what you are doing, really, or what you are like.

Yet when you draw back and look at yourself, you can perceive many imperfections which you wouldn't have seen otherwise.

Text inspired by The Mother (Mirra Alfassa)

We are not only what we know of ourselves but an immense more which we do not know; our momentary personality is only a bubble on the ocean of our existence. – Sri Aurobindo, The Life Divine

I am not my thoughts.

A quiet mind does not mean that there will be no thoughts or mental movements at all, but that these will be on the surface, and you will feel your true being within, separate from them, observing but not carried away.

Sri Aurobindo

Day 15: Holding Space

Can I hold space for myself?

Can I walk alongside myself, whatever journey I am on, without judging myself?

When I judge myself I make myself feel inadequate.

Often, as a result, I try to fix myself.

When this is what keeps me busy, I am cut off from being in the flow of life.

When self rests in the space of Self, my heart stays open.

There is a sense of unlimited unconditional support which, in turn, allows me to let go of judgment and control.

Often, we are prone to judging ourselves or others.

If we judge others, it normally means we also judge ourselves, perhaps even more harshly.

> *Forgiveness is not something we do for other people. We do it for ourselves to get well and move on.*
> – LiveLifeHappy.com

Clear Space and Invite Yourself

Find your favourite quiet spot, at home or wherever you can be undisturbed. Sit in a comfortable position. Close your eyes and imagine the wisest and most loving version of yourself sitting opposite.

Engage in a dialogue with this version of yourself.

Imagine, you have the most amazing listener at the ready, just for you!

How does the conversation go?

Keep in mind that accepting and forgiving ourselves can open us up to Self Love.

Write down the conversation here.

Day 16: Monkey Mind Rules

Our 'monkey mind' controls us without us even being aware of it.

Dramas unfold and we are dragged along, at least as long as we identify with the thoughts and corresponding emotions.

No longer the witness, we become the victim.

When we become the victim, we feel that we are being chased down a dark and never-ending tunnel.

We see no separation between our circumstances and who we are.

That is the illusion from which we need to break out.

Instead of letting our thoughts control us, we need to control them, ideally becoming aware of the very moment a thought appears.

We are not our thoughts and we can choose to let the thoughts sail on by.

Take Back the Power

Sit with your hands in front of your chest, palms open, slightly cupped and facing the ceiling. Visualise your most unwanted repeat-thought landing in the palms of your hands, then blow the thought away.

Imagine that an empowering and joyful thought takes its place. Smile.

How do you feel?

Make a note of your empowering thought, emotions and feelings.

Day 17: Glossing Over

There is a lot to read about manifesting an ideal life through visualisation.

This, by default, means to paint an all-positive picture.

No doubt visualisation can be a great tool, though living in accordance with our higher self can only truly manifest when we accept all aspects of ourselves.

Anything that remains rejected, hidden away, or denied, will hinder, or even hijack, our aspirations.

Accepting all facets of ourselves, fully and completely, on the other hand - neither denying nor 'glossing over' - is hugely empowering, although it can feel scary and debilitating.

There is no way around and no leaving out, we have to integrate all aspects of ourselves, incorporate and bring them along, passing through, whilst remaining the observer of them all.

Accept, Integrate and Move On

Sit in a comfortable position, with the backs of your hands resting on your knees. Bring to mind whatever it is, if anything, that you (still) find unacceptable about yourself.

Vow to leave this unwanted aspect behind or take it by your hand and walk together on the path.

Make some notes here of "the unacceptable", and see if you can make peace with this aspect, fully accept it as part of yourself, or if you can overcome and leave it in the past.

Day 18: When the Going Gets Tough...

Our inner progress becomes extra visible whenever we experience difficulties or hardship, because our progress can be measured by how calm we remain.

> *The people you meet are either a reflection of a repeated cycle or guides towards a new start. Notice the difference.*
> *– Conscious Awakening*

To remain calm means we are not trying to control what is happening. Instead we remain the witness of what is happening. It's a kind of surrender, and it's the best alternative when feeling impatient, anxious, or fearful. It means to 'let go and let God'.

The perceived hardship can be that we are not receiving something, or someone, that we wish to receive. To surrender doesn't mean we can't wish for things to happen, but to do so with full trust, accepting the outcome whatever it may be. If we wish for something to happen with impatience or desperation, surely fear is at play.

... The Tough Keep Calm

Sitting in an inspiring space, invite into your mind the formulation of what it is, right now, that you desire the most.

No matter the want, are you set on 'getting it', or do you feel OK with whatever might come?

Keep in mind that even if you feel that having this desire fulfilled will bring you towards your life purpose, the point is that if it 'ruffles you' not to 'get it', no matter how well-intended the desire, it is rather teaching you something about your inability to insist on getting 'what you want' – much like a child throwing a tantrum, and this must always be ego.

Feeling your inspiration write down what you desire most.

Day 19: Staying Stuck

Humans are conditioned to see the world in a certain way. We often look at it as being either black or white.

Our sense of self is continuously reinforced through our beliefs.

Rarely do we choose to step back and examine the belief system that we have unconsciously adopted over the years.

Protective patterns help validate our beliefs. They are our 'default setting' and help us feel safe.

For example, we think that we are smart when we defend our viewpoints.

The truth is that reality - as most of us believe it to exist - is only a projection of our minds.

And each time we reaffirm our perception, we miss an opportunity to get just that little bit closer to real freedom and our true essence.

Morning Ritual: Joy at Dawn

Ideally at the break of dawn or anytime in the morning, lie or sit quietly and fully focused inwards. Do this on Day 20.

Remind yourself that although you may not be able to control what will happen to you during the day, you have the power over how you will react to whatever comes your way.

Vow to remember this for the whole morning and the remainder of the day. Vow to be conscious.

Make some notes about your reactions to whatever was coming your way during the day, at the end of the day.

Day 20: Seeking Guidance

A friend, healer or coach can help us look within to find answers. Often we find a lot of release by sharing. At other times it can be scary to seek help, and to expose our own private realm.

The path of healing is almost never 'plain sailing'. It requires truthfulness and honesty.

It's hard enough to speak honestly to ourselves, let alone to someone else.

And as we start to transform, the ego kicks in. It rebels, fighting for its own existence. Ego wants to survive; it doesn't want to let go.

The natural reaction when this happens is to blame somebody else. It is easy to find targets amongst the people that surround us. Even the healer might get accused.

We might say that so and so is not treating us well or doesn't understand us.

This offers a way out. Allowing for this to happen, means we could miss a whole new world view opening up to us.

Start with Gratitude

Sit in a quiet space, in a comfortable position. Bring to mind a friend, healer or any person who has helped you along on your path to greater self-acceptance and understanding. Send her/him your gratitude.

Ask yourself what guidance you are seeking as you move on with your life, your next project, your job, health, relationship... and who could help you.

Even if unclear or vague, jot down some notes here.

Day 21: Surrendering

Understand that many of the energy-draining efforts to improve yourself, to figure things out or to plan for faraway goals, are not worth their while.

Most people spend their whole lives using their strengths to cover up and hide their weaknesses. They expend tremendous energy in keeping themselves a house divided. But if you surrender to your weakness, therein lies your pathway to genius. – Moshe Feldenkrais

As you surrender to the wishes of the universe and what is happening in your life, you will experience the miracles that the universe is able to concoct, and how it's doing a much better job of it than you ever could. Remember: the universe wants you just as you are, right now.

Be what you are, as you are. If in this process all your weaknesses and imperfections come to the front and people lose their respect for you, don't let it bother you. You are sincere and that sincerity will make you progress.

Arrive at Self Love

Drawing is one form of creative expression, and as with all forms of creative expression we tap in to whatever awareness is ready to emerge from deep within.

For this assignment, make sure that you have some colour pencils or water colours, paint brushes, and a cup of water within reach.

Create a colour drawing or painting depicting your transition from trying to control your life to surrendering, feeling at peace.

Paint whatever comes; it can be something concrete or abstract. In this drawing/painting, is there a particular detail or colour that can be said to represent Self Love?

Self Love is not selfish; you cannot truly love another until you know how to love yourself. – Riya Arora

Week 4
In Everyday Life

Your Lord is within you,
Like fragrance in the flowers.
Why, like a musk deer
Are you searching for musk
in the grass
again and again
- Kabir

You might want to replace the word 'Lord' with 'soul' – with no disrespect to Kabir!

In Everyday Life

"In the Himalayas there is a small deer, commonly called the musk deer. The male of the species has a small gland under its tail. During the mating season, this gland secretes a scent that is so heady and powerful that the deer himself goes a bit wild trying to locate its source, never realizing that he, himself, is that source.

We have been trained all our lives to look without. To watch the world that we might gather enough success, money, love and safety to finally be happy. Of course it never works in any lasting fashion.

What we are looking for is within us. It always has been, it always will be. It is the field from which the success of our life arises. It is the source, course and goal of all the love that we seek and seek to express. It is the ultimate safety because it is the Truth. That which never changes. And its very nature is bliss. True happiness that is based on nothing other than our acceptance of it.

We simply need to look to ourselves - past all the thoughts and feelings and stresses of any given moment - to see it here.

Like fragrance in the flowers."

Jeff Kober

Day 22: Words Carry an Emotional Charge

Everything we hear or read carries an emotional charge. The word 'death' evokes a different type of sensation in our body than the word 'love' does, for example. Most often we are not aware of the reaction in our body, but we can start to become more conscious. Brick by brick we can build a bridge from mind to body.

Today, we are drowning in information. Hooked on it, we continuously overload our minds with information, almost subconsciously.

Sometimes we see it as part of the task at hand. We want to stay 'up to date'. This is often driven by a Fear Of Missing Out (FOMO), or we want to achieve some tangible outcome that makes us shine in the eyes of others.

At other times we are seeking temporary relief and indulge in entertainment e.g. on social media, out of a fear of feeling bored.

When this is all happening without any sense of a higher purpose it can harm us.

Practice Self Discipline

Practice reading different words and becoming aware of the accompanying sensation in your body.

Pen your thoughts about what is happening in your body as you read these words:

- Climate Change
- Peace
- War
- Health
- Love

Pledge to be aware of the sensations in your body when you hear or read different words, as often as you can remember.

Choose some other words which come into your mind and feel their emotional charge.

Day 23: Where does Time Go?

We ask ourselves, where did the day go? This is a natural reaction when it seems like time is flying by.

It might help us to remind ourselves of our purpose, and if we don't feel that we have one, to make it a priority to find out why we are here, in this body, on this earth.

Time is limited, indeed, and we owe it to our soul - not our ego personality - to discover and live our unique soul purpose.

If this seems an impossible task, one might consider that, in life, there are no coincidences and that everything that happens is meant to happen.

So, if my soul chose this very life with all its peculiarities and hardship, what does it mean?

What is it telling me to do?

Does it perhaps have the power to shift me out of a place of needs or desires to a space of gratitude and joy, in the moment?

Set Your Intention

For each of the following, write a summary of the past and an intention for the future. If you want to be more detailed than this space allows, take an additional sheet of paper and write as much as you feel like writing. Intention setting is a part of activating your receptivity for the experience.

Your life

Summary:

Intention:

Continued on the next page

This Year

Summary:

Intention:

Today

Summary:

Intention:

Right at this very moment

Summary:

Intention:

Day 24: Conscious Sleep

On this day, read this in the evening, at bedtime, instead of in the morning.

Spend a few minutes before falling asleep. Lie on your back and imagine that light is streaming into your body, then ask your higher self to protect, heal and guide you during your sleep.

Also, ask your subconscious to guide you regarding any particular question that you have.

Express the question!

Request that as you wake up in the morning, you will be aware of your very first thought.

Finally, make sure that the journal is by your bedside for the morning, in order to be ready to do the assignment then (you may already want to read the instruction).

Catch the First Thought (do this on Day 25)

The reason why life is a sleep and dream for most people is because their awareness is caught up with past or future and not with what is.
– Deepak Chopra

As you wake up, open your eyes and remain still in bed. Lying on your back, zoom in on your very first thought; you may become aware of a dream that you had, or any other thought might pop into your mind. Whatever it is, be aware, pay attention to it.

Note down the first thought of the day:

What does it tell you? Is it providing you with any guidance regarding the question you posed just before sleeping?

Are there any accompanying sensations in the body? Make some notes here (and then move on to the instruction for Day 25, or leave it for later in the day).

Day 25: Rise and Shine

We all know that life will end one day.

We also know that we should be living each day with joy and happiness, grateful to be alive.

As long as this remains the kind of knowledge that resides in the mind, nothing will change for the better.

We may think that we know 'it'. However as the creatures of habit that we have become we go about our lives as if life is never-ending, and struggle to feel joy.

We try hard to feel joy.

Some things work better than others.

Walks in nature, massage, body movement, and deep listening can all do wonders.

They have the potential to teach us to truly embrace a state of happiness and fulfilment.

Joy is the truth of our being.

Experiencing true joy can help us transcend to higher frequencies of being.

Let Go

Dance and movement are excellent tools for letting go of energies that no longer serve you. Music and dance have the power to soothe, balance, liberate and elevate.

To allow your body to let go of tensions, put on some sacred music and tune in to your body. Stretch your body, feel it and experience the energies pulsating.

Breathe and stay witness to any strong emotions.

Let yourself shake, wiggle and get low down on the floor... Crawl, shake your hips, swing your arms... allow whatever wants to emerge... How does it feel?

You may want to choose from this list of Sacred Songs available on YouTube:

- Prophecy Song - Joanne Shenandoah - Peace and Power
- Peia Luzzi - Blessed We Are
- En el Cielo (Pacha Mama) - Nessi Gome (Isabel Ruiz cover)
- Tina Turner - Sarvesham Svastir Bhavatu (Peace Mantra)
- I am the light of my soul - Sirgun Kaur and Sat Darshan Singh
- Curawake - He Yama Yo
- Mooji Music - Shiva Shambo
- Asatoma - Kevin James Carroll
- Om Namah Shivaya - Krishna Das Live
- Kiss the Earth (La Luna) - Ajeet Kaur
- Fia - Shine (studio version)

Day 26: Body, Mind and Spirit

We look at ourselves as separate people moving around in a world that is separate from us. We feel limited. Even within our own bodies we often feel trapped or separated.

Most of us live without acknowledging the unison of body, mind and spirit. We criticize our body expecting it to do whatever it is that we want. The moment it develops an ailment or disease, we are shocked, disappointed. We may even be angry.

> *You are not a drop in the ocean.*
> *You are the entire ocean in a drop.*
> *– Rumi*

Allowing our heads to stay in control, we stubbornly pursue whatever it is that our beliefs and conditioning tell us to.

Often we chase after success or recognition and monetary riches, when the truth is that we are vast beyond our greatest imagination.

Only when living with body, mind and spirit united in the awareness of unconditional love, are we truly living.

Feeling vast, as we are, reduces all the stresses and difficulties that we may be experiencing.

Imagine Your Vastness

Imagine the sky or the ocean or a vast field and vow to identify with it, to become one with it, entering into it.

Ask, imagine and/or feel the sky or the ocean or the vast field entering into you.

Merge with its vastness.

How does it feel? What do you sense? (Perhaps the opposite of feeling small, or that nothing is separate?)

Make some notes here.

Day 27: Embodying Joy

We easily let mindsets and stubborn patterns run our lives. These can centre on work, home, relationships... and offer a sense of comfort, or discomfort.

As we start to walk the path of self-discovery we often feel a desire to shift ourselves into new, fresh and more wholesome ways of being. For example, loosening up and being able to laugh at ourselves can truly help.

Rituals can support our settling into new patterns and to remaining connected to our joy. And remember, if we make excuses like 'I don't have time', we are not prioritising our own happiness.

We delight in the beauty of the butterfly, but rarely admit the changes it has gone through to achieve that beauty. - Maya Angelou

When we care for the connection to ourselves we allow for new feelings and thoughts to reach our consciousness.

Implement Rituals for Connection

Assess your daily patterns and rituals, checking in with your inner being. What, if anything, wants to change? Maybe you'd like there to be more playfulness and joy - whatever it means to you - in your life? How could you make it so, ideally on a daily basis?

A ritual can provide you with a focal point and an opportunity to demonstrate reverence for being in the moment. Rituals can elevate your physical and emotional consciousness and attune you with the source of your creation.

Here are some Ideas for Rituals

Walk in nature, any green and open space will do. Noticing the patterns on the leaves of the trees, allow yourself to step back from your usual busy (or whichever word fits) self. Hug a tree, touch a flower, or walk barefoot in the grass or on a sandy beach. Feel the connection to mother earth, feel the soil or create a sacred space in your home.

Consider implementing a daily ritual that helps you reconnect to the sacred space within you. What ritual are you drawn to? Feel into yourself.

Day 28: I Am

I am more than my body.

I am more than my thoughts.

I am more than my emotions.

I am also less than all those things.

I am, without any of those things.

I am Creation.

I am one with the Creator.

I am the Creator.

I am no thing. I surrender. I pray. I bow.

Even forgetting it, I am.

Creating a life experience in alignment with our soul purpose requires that we make conscious choices and sometimes that we fundamentally change our beliefs and the way that we look at life and ourselves in it.

The above text may seem strange and we may want a logical explanation of it. We can also try to surrender and just let the words sink in.

True freedom requires perseverance to transform our own limitations; it's a journey of the heart.

It is the journey to Self Love.
– Claudia Roth

Tune In

Connect to your body with three deep breaths by holding the in-breath for a few seconds before each exhalation.

Without judging, feel whatever sensations are arising in your body.

What is shifting within you? Who are you today, and who do you want to be tomorrow? Knowing that what you truly are - Love, Bliss, Self - lies beneath the changing persona, which offers a deeply felt Joy.

Write here about your contemplation.

The Story behind this journal. What next?

By Claudia Roth

In my case, it was when I found myself at the Sri Aurobindo Ashram in Pondicherry that a clear fork in the road started to form. I was on a business trip to India, and a colleague had set me up with what I assumed was a business meeting. Still focused on business and my career, I thought that I was there to sell luxury hotels. Sadly, that was pretty much the only thing I knew at the time. I soon realised that other kinds of business and luxury were on the agenda - those concerned with self-transformation.

In that Ashram - a rather unusual environment for the kind of career-minded senior executive that I was - I was asked the 4 profound questions included as part of the 7th day assignment of this journal. At the time, I was unable to answer in the spirit intended. Thinking in the language of the soul was something completely new to me. I was travelling on the highway of life. Fast-moving and efficient, I was fully focused on pursuing my career.

A vague notion told me that I was about to depart from that highway, that a new journey had begun. That feeling has only grown stronger with time, especially as I met a stranger called Vijay in the forest in Auroville, a spiritual community in the south of India. And the quest for Self goes on... I hope that you enjoy Your Journey as much as I am enjoying mine.

In full gratitude for the unconditional love and support of my support of my husband, my parents, teachers and friends and with love, gratitude and my blessings to you all.

Claudia Roth

Do check back to Soul Luxury's website for my fictionalised spiritual memoir that tells the story.

For something more hands on, I offer Quantum Energy Coaching (QEC) in one-to-one sessions. QEC is a simple and powerful tool to 'delete' self-limiting beliefs and 'install' more positive ones on the subconscious.

I facilitate workshops and as a speaker I wish to inspire others to live life as an expression of Self Love. Be Love - Spread Love. For more information visit www.soul-luxury.com

Next? Keep Going!

Knowing how the mind works, you are perhaps wondering how to keep going?

One way: Simply intend to keep an open heart and trust that life will point out the way.

And: Plan a special activity for yourself to celebrate having undertaken this journaling journey, and "simply" for being alive today. The activity, of course, may be nothing but a day of doing nothing, of just being with yourself.

If you feel like it, you may re-do this very journaling journey again. At a later point in your life, I bet you will note the shifts that have happened for you since the last time around. Remember that future self? It will be as if another person altogether is doing the work, because it is. Your awareness will have evolved and you will read and respond to things differently. The only constant is change.

Trust me, you will know what to do and somehow it will just happen, as opposed to you engineering it all.

Some thought she fell into madness for the way she changed. She thought it was madness to live the life she once did. – JmStorm

Acknowledgement

This journal has been made possible given the unconditional support from very special people in my life! I feel deeply privileged, humble and honoured for your support in my journey sharing the Truth - from ego to Self Love.

From my heart I thank you all for your love. We are all One. We are all love.

Your Self Love Notes

www.ingramcontent.com/pod-product-compliance
Ingram Content Group UK Ltd.
Pitfield, Milton Keynes, MK11 3LW, UK
UKHW060117010826
14089UKWH00004B/32

9 781916 350700